WESTWARD

WESTWARD

POEMS BY

AMY CLAMPITT

ALFRED A. KNOPF
NEW YORK
1990

THIS IS A BORZOI BOOK
PUBLISHED BY ALFRED A. KNOPF, INC.

Copyright © 1990 by Amy Clampitt

All rights reserved under International and Pan-American Copyright Conventions. Published in the United States by Alfred A.
Knopf, Inc., New York, and simultaneously in Canada by Random House of Canada Limited, Toronto. Distributed by Random
House, Inc., New York.

Acknowledgments for previously published poems are to be found
on page 107.

Library of Congress Cataloging-in-Publication Data

Clampitt, Amy.
    Westward:poems/by Amy Clampitt.—1st ed.
        p.   cm.
    ISBN 0-394-58455-4
    ISBN 0-679-72867-8 (pbk.)
    I. Title.
PS3553.L23W47   1990
811'.54—dc20   89-43359
                                       CIP

Manufactured in the United States of America
First Edition

TO THE MEMORY
OF MY PARENTS
AND MY GRANDPARENTS

. . . And bade it to the East
Be faithful . . .

EMILY DICKINSON

CONTENTS

I CROSSINGS

II HABITATS

III   A SORT OF FOOTHOLD

IV   THE PRAIRIE

I

CROSSINGS

JOHN DONNE IN CALIFORNIA

Is the Pacific Sea my home? Or is
Jerusalem? pondered John Donne,
who never stood among these strenuous,
huge, wind-curried hills, their green
gobleted just now with native poppies'
opulent red-gold, where New World lizards run
among strange bells, thistles wear the guise
of lizards, and one shining oak is poison;

or cast an eye on lofted strong-arm
redwoods' fog-fondled silhouette,
their sapling wisps among the ferns in time
more his (perhaps) than our compeer: here at
the round earth's numbly imagined rim,
its ridges drowned in the irradiating vat
of evening, the land ends; the magnesium
glare whose unbridged nakedness is bright

beyond imagining, begins. John Donne,
I think, would have been more at home
than the frail wick of metaphor I've brought
to see by, and cannot, for the conflagration
of this nightfall's utter strangeness.

MEADOWLARK COUNTRY

FOR DORIS THOMPSON MYERS

Speaking of the skylark in a New England classroom—
nonbird, upward-twirler, Old-World hyperbole—
I thought how the likewise ground-nesting
Western meadowlark, rather than soar unsupported
out over the cattle range at daybreak, takes up
its post on a fencepost. I heard them out there,
once, by the hundreds, one after another:
a liquid millennium arising from the still
eastward-looking venue of the dark—

like the still-evolving venue of the young, the faces
eastward-looking, bright with a mute,
estranged, ancestral puzzlement.

4

NOTES ON THE STATE OF VIRGINIA

Ground fog blurring the dogwood,
black haw, sweet gum, sassafras
and hickory along the waterways,
the branches overhead so full
of warblers on the move toward
destinations, habitats they're

ignorant of any need to find
their way to, to explore,
exploit, alter the face of:
prevailing winds, disheveled
shores, the wet brink's tidal
waverings: the branches overhead

so full of small, unfrightened
quicknesses that if you shook
them they'd simply flutter free
in loosened gusts, ink-straked,
eye-ringed, wing-barred, marked
or cowled with dark, or vivid as

these loosening streams—oxblood,
crimson, flame, clear yellow—
from the already stripped, half
stark, half still gorgeous wood-
lands we glimpse in passing.
Glooming through fog, the cypress,

up to its knees in tidal muck,
will likewise stand bare under
the winter rains. The burnished
tenacity of holly and magnolia, the
scissored undercroft of boxwood,
look like permanence. Ringingly,

the mockingbird—a virtuoso in
and out of season—declares
it lives here, unsubjected
to prevailing winds or tides, to
anything it chooses not to notice:
laws, controls, confederations

don't faze its self-assertive
stances: not the stocks, the
statehouse with the Union Jack atop
it, church every Sunday, monuments,
earthworks, battlefields, the vague
repositories of the dead. Upwards

of forty different tribes. . . having
never submitted themselves to any
laws, any coercive power. . . . Were it
made a question, whether no law
or too much law. . . submits man
to the greatest evil, one who

has seen both conditions of
existence would pronounce it
(thus Jefferson) to be the last.
The mockingbird, an opportunist
ready to expand its range where
there's an opening, lives well,

sings in all weathers, gives no
heed to the accustomary collection
of bones, and deposition of them,
in barrows (since obliterated)
by parties moving through the
country, whose expressions were

construed to be those of sorrow:
ignorant of royal grants, crests,
charters, sea power, mercantile
expansion, the imperative to
find an opening, explore, exploit,
and in so doing begin to alter,

with its straking smudge and smear,
little by little, this opening in
the foliage, wet brink of all our
enterprise: the blur of bays, the
estuarial fog at sunrise, the glooms
and glimmerings, the tidal waters.

KUDZU DORMANT

Ropes, pulleys, shawls,
caparisons, tent curtains
the hue of mildew, strung
above the raw, red-gulleyed
wintering hide of Dixie—

rambunctious eyesore,
entrepreneur (as most are)
from away off somewhere,
like the overdressed though
feral daffodils that prosper

under burnt-out chimneys, in
middens, lethargies, debris
of enterprise that's slipped
into the lap of yet another
annal of the poor: deplore

it dormant or, on principle,
admire it green, a panacea
rampant is what's muscled
in—a charming strangler
setting the usual example.

THE FIELD PANSY

Yesterday, just before the first frost of the season,
I discovered a violet in bloom on the lawn—a white one,
with a mesh of faint purple pencil marks above the hollow
at the throat, where the petals join: an irregular, a waif,
out of sync with the ubiquity of the asters of New England,

or indeed with the johnny-jump-ups I stopped to look at,
last week, in a plot by the sidewalk: weedily prolific
common garden perennial whose lineage goes back to
the bi- or tri-colored native field pansy of Europe:
ancestor of the cloned ocher and aubergine, the cream-white,

the masked motley, the immaculate lilac-blue of the pansies
that thrive in the tended winter plots of tidewater Virginia,
where in spring the cutover fields at the timber's edge,
away from the boxwood and magnolia alleys, are populous
with an indigenous, white, just faintly suffused-with-violet

first cousin: a link with what, among the hollows of the
great dunes of Holland, out of reach of the slide and hurl
of the North Sea breakers, I found growing a summer ago—a
field pansy tinged not violet but pink, sometimes approaching
the hue of the bell of a foxglove: a gathering, a proliferation

on a scale that, for all its unobtrusiveness, seems to be
worldwide, of what I don't know how to read except as an
urge to give pleasure: a scale that may, for all our fazed
dubiety, indeed be universal. I know I'm leaving something out
when I write of this omnipresence of something like eagerness,

this gushing insouciance that appears at the same time capable
of an all but infinite particularity: sedulous, patient, though
in the end (so far as anyone can see) without consequence.
What is consequence? What difference do the minutiae
of that seeming inconsequence that's called beauty

add up to? Life was hard in the hinterland, where spring arrived
with a gush of violets, sky-blue out of the ground of the woodlot,
but where a woman was praised by others of her sex for being
Practical, and by men not at all, other than in a slow reddening
about the neck, a callowly surreptitious wolf-whistle: where the mode

was stoic, and embarrassment stood in the way of affect:
a mother having been alarmingly seen in tears, once only
we brought her a fistful of johnny-jump-ups from the garden,
"because you were crying"—and saw we'd done the wrong thing.

DALLAS-FORT WORTH:
REDBUD AND MISTLETOE

Terrain that from above, aboard the hurled
steel spore, appears suffused with vivid
ravelings, the highways' mimic of veinings

underground, the fossil murk we're all
propelled by, for whatever term: as with
magenta freshets of Texas redbud, curled

among dun oaks fed on by yellowing nuggets
of old mistletoe, the sometime passport
to sulphurous Avernus (*the golden leafage*

rustling in light wind), though here we hugely
deafen to the hiss of Nemesis: *so turns*
the wheel of change; so turns the world.

DELETED PASSAGE

In the dead of January, while snow fell
dwindling, a lisp inside a drafty flue,
lying in bed alone I dreamed of furnaces.
At the bland beginning there were conferees
in a hired room, the scrape of folding chairs,
a chartered bus, and then a border crossed,
a meadow in another climate: deep
in that alien grass, I turned and saw
and recognized at once—changed, strange,
unrecognizable—a friend long dead,
instantaneity of dreaming fusing
fluidity and rigor, the once child-hater
become a shepherdess of children—nymphets
with madonna faces, their long hair flowing
as they ran, as they came racing
through the foreign grass
to offer us, with all the pampered charm
of their estate, the keys: we sat with them
in kitchens and at secret tables,
knowing ourselves beguiled.
                         And then a change.
There is something I have forgotten: how or why
we are once more on the move, and who is at the wheel
here in the dark, the thrilling foreign dark.
But what, having veered from the ordinary way,
we are seeing, what we are being shown,
is privileged: there is someone
who does not and who must not know
we have been witnesses of what we are now
witness to: dome after dome

along the secret road, enceinte
with scarlet, licking maws.
                              It is too late.
I have looked, I have seen
the stokers hunkering. It is too late
now to unthink the worst.

SEDER NIGHT

When he lost his way in the Hagodah
        they knew: a year from then
the moonlight traveling the bedclothes
        would find him gone.

Rooftop-occluded, the Passover moonrise
        shrinks to a talisman;
memory's thumbed-over congeries,
        year by year, wears down,

goes bald, loses its smell, its senses
        to the denomination of a coin,
a pair of cufflinks in a drawer,
        a wedding photograph, a son—

an only son, an offshoot of the larger
        process of uprooting
from the shtetl, the movement westward—
        the ritual yearning:

Jerusalem: assimilations, dispersals,
        furnaces: Never again!
The vacated bedclothes, the rising of
        the seasonal moon.

MULCIBER AT WEST EGG

*. . . headlong sent
with his industrious crew to build in hell.*
PARADISE LOST, BOOK I

An old man bundled into a long ulster
who'd telegraphed and then taken the day coach
from somewhere in Minnesota, having read
about what happened in the papers—"it was all
in the Chicago papers. I started right away"—

Henry C. Gatz, seduced out of his grief
by the arts of Mulciber, now looked about him
and saw for the first time the light and splendor
of the place, rooms opening into other rooms.
"If he'd of lived, he'd of been another

James J. Hill," the old man told Nick Carraway.
No, he didn't want to take the body West.
"He rose to his position in the East.
If he'd of lived . . ." It isn't Gatsby
but his daddy, the unlegendary Henry C.,

who daunts me: docile, unpresentable, bewildered,
not even a has-been, just a never-was-much
out of the past, the sticks, the shtetl,
clinging to each and every one of us who ever
meanly dazzled an un-up-to-date sure loser

with What's What. "He rose to his position
in the East": built a show place, lived
in splendor, and for all whom fiction
cannot disabuse, his fall—no Hurstwood
on the dole—is as the fall of Lucifer.

AT A REST STOP IN OHIO

Forth from the hand
of God, or, proximately,
the cavern of a westbound

Greyhound, the little
simple soul, at no
great distance still

from its scathed and
shivering first cry,
its gasping first, blind

mouthful, here and now
wallows howling, as
though there were no

elsewhere: What ails it?
The dark night of the
little simple soul, without

so much as the resources
to demand to know
Why was I born? is

dark indeed. Bound though
it may be for the city
of the angels, snow

warnings intervene,
to discommode a mother
ebony of cheekbone

and more than comely
but listless to realign
the warp of history by

more than a snippet, or
forestall, when the wailing
stops, the looming torpor—

except from, just possibly,
inside the fragile
ambush of being funny.

IOLA, KANSAS

Riding all night, the bus half empty, toward the interior,
among refineries, trellised and turreted illusory cities,
the crass, the indispensable wastefulness of oil rigs
offshore, of homunculi swigging at the gut of a continent:

the trailers, the semis, the vans, the bumper stickers,
slogans in day-glo invoking the name of Jesus, who knows
what it means: the air waves, the brand name, the backyard
Barbie-doll barbecue, graffiti in video, the burblings,

the dirges: *heart like a rock, I said Kathy I'm lost,*
the scheme is a mess, we've left Oklahoma, its cattle,
sere groves of pecan trees interspersing the horizonless
belch and glare, the alluvium of the auto junkyards,

we're in Kansas now, we've turned off the freeway,
we're meandering, as again night falls, among farmsteads,
the little towns with the name of a girl on the watertower,
the bandstand in the park at the center, the churches

alight from within, perpendicular banalities of glass
candy-streaked purple-green-yellow (who is this Jesus?),
the strangeness of all there is, whatever it is, growing
stranger, we've come to a rest stop, the name of the girl

on the watertower is Iola: no video, no vending machines,
but Wonder Bread sandwiches, a pie: "It's boysenberry,
I just baked it today," the woman behind the counter
believably says, the innards a purply glue, and I eat it

with something akin to reverence: free refills from
the Silex on the hot plate, then back to our seats,
the loud suction of air brakes like a thing alive, and
the voices, the sleeping assembly raised, as by an agency

out of the mystery of the interior, to a community—
and through some duct in the rock I feel my heart go out,
out here in the middle of nowhere (the scheme is a mess)
to the waste, to the not knowing who or why, and am happy.

ANTIPHONAL

Passed and repassed on the way to Vespers,
a nun-cultivated rose, day-vivid
exemplar of things not seen, concurs

with not only the primordial snuffler
at the root but, also, the apprehension
lodged no one can say precisely where,

of an expanding state of being, tier
on beatific tier, that's entered only
by the strait stairwell of the ear:

the antiphonal, the as-though-single
exhalation of an entire community
informs the hollow, paired, frail,

seashell-like neighbor to the brain's
immured and numerable corridors
with inklings of an omnipresence,

a not-yet-imaginable solstice
past that footstone (O terror)
the unsupported senses cannot cross.

A NOTE FROM LEYDEN

Rain-drenched, Rhine-drained,
cobbled, moated, durable: an all
but innumerable multitude of eardrums
played on by centuries of
chink and clatter, the downpour
from bell tower and flèche
above the flatland: the fragile
polder, each green stanza of
its made earth metrical,
the watery hem, the duneland
pocked, unstable, flowery—
pools at nightfall harbored in
ghost-wineries of evening primrose,
the daylight tremulous,
the North Sea vapors a towering
tumid purple or a slack, ungirdled,
silksack impermanence: nuanced,
cloudbanklike dishevelings
of silver poplar, the undersides
of willows mercurial above
the waterways, a colloquy
with something tugged at
elsewhere, otherwise:
    Arise, arise
and to your scattered bodies go . . .
Out of the hinterland an already
halfway disembodied circumstance,
out of the fleeing, the reckless
habitat of past sensation: *All*
whom the flood did . . .

The flood,
an inkling of it: far from this
moated, painterly estrangement
a night of roaring, the morning
dimly sodden: never had there been
such rain—the creek below the garden
swollen, sheeted, the willow foliage
we'd unimaginably played in the shade of
a muddied den of drowning. *Whom
the flood did, and fire shall
o'erthrow* . . .

Not elsewhere,
not otherwise: in that same
hinterland, one schoolday a sick
lilac haze that came, they said,
from forests burning somewhere
to the north. (How far? I'd never
seen a forest.) On the morrow
a bleared thickening, the whole
world gone yellow. At noon
schoolbuses came to take us home.
Such dark, such howling under
the sun, was Biblical. John Donne
had not considered dust storms. Nor
had, here in Leyden, William Brewster,
with his flock of souls. The Dutch
from their drenched enclave at
the brink of empire could not
have done so. And we? We were,
and did not know we were, the future
no forefather could precisely, could
even flickeringly foresee.

HAVING LUNCH AT BRASENOSE

Possible by now, one would suppose,
to look out, coming down from London,
at the wheatfield poppies, the dogrose
    and elder, the water meadows,

and after the foursquare nightmare
of cooling towers at Didcot, again
at the occluded, sliding signature
    of domes, finials and spires,

with no particular pang or tremor
for what one had been—irretrievably,
it seemed then to a dazed latecomer—
    so long ago undone by:

the burgeoning of stone, the shiver
everywhere—it was spring, with the
English chill, and one was very young—
    of the longstanding:

sequesterer of such carelessness,
such poise, lit up by the dazzling
gaze of him with whom one was, of
    course, at once in love

overwhelmingly, cravenly half aware
even then it was no merely erotic
trap one had fallen into, it was
    centuries of enclosure,

it was the walls, not the riotous
break-in of all that was happening,
mainly, in one's own imagination:
　　the fact of brass,

the shapeliness, the perpendicular
heft of the Bodleian, the Radcliffe Camera's
hovering poise, yes, and the hard nose
　　of the eponymous

brazen lion one has now the luck
of another look at, decades later—
to uncover, lodged in a bedrock
　　older than marble or

the bronze of monuments, this
brazen waif, this changeling—
the intransigeance, the airy
　　indignity of being young.

WESTWARD

FOR ANTHONY KEMP

Distance is dead. At Gatwick, at Heathrow
the loud spoor, the grinding tremor,
manglings, accelerated trade routes

in reverse: the flyblown exotic place,
the heathen shrine exposed. A generation
saw it happen: the big-eyed, spindling

overleapers of the old slow silk route
shiver in terylene at Euston, grimed
caravansary of dispersal, where a lone

pigeon circles underneath the girders,
trapped in the breaking blur of sound waves—
a woman's sourceless voice interminably

counting off the terminals, a sibyl's
lapful of uncertainties. There's trouble
to the north, the trains are late: from

knotted queues the latest émigrés
of a spent Commonwealth look up: so many,
drawn toward what prospect, from what

point of origin? Bound for Iona in
the Western Isles, doleful, unlulled
by British Rail, lying awake I listen

to the clicking metronome as time
runs out, feeling the old assumptions,
aired, worm-tunneled, crumble,

thinking of the collapse of distance:
Proust's paradise of the unvisited,
of fool's-gold El Dorado. At Glasgow

there's still trouble, but the train
to Oban's running. Rain seeps in;
past the streaked, streaming pane,

a fir-fringed, sodden glimpse, the
verberation of a name: Loch Lomond.
"Really?" The callow traveler opposite

looks up, goes back to reading—yes,
it really is Thucydides: hubris,
brazen entitlements, forepangs of

letting go, all that. At Oban, a wet
trek to the ferry landing, where a
nun, or the daft counterfeit of one

(time runs out, the meek grow jaded,
shibboleths of piety no guarantee):
veil and wimple above dank waterproof,

nun-blue pantsuit protruding—lugs
half a dozen satchels ("tinned things
you can't get up here"), has misplaced

her ticket, is so fecklessly egregious
it can't (or could it, after all?) be
contraband. From Craignure, Isle of Mull,

a bus jolts westward, traversing, and
it's still no picnic, the slow route
Keats slogged through on that wet

walking tour: a backward-looking
homage, not a setting forth, as for
his brother George, into the future:

drowned Lycidas, whether beyond the
stormy . . . And of course it rained,
the way it's doing as I skitter up

the cleated iron of the gangway at
Fionnphort; Iona, an indecipherable
blur, a slosh of boots and oilskins,

once landed on, is even wetter.
Not that it always rains: tomorrow
everything will be diaphanous

as the penumbra of a jellyfish:
I'll ride to Staffa over tourmaline
and amethyst without a wrinkle;

will stand sun-warmed above the bay
where St. Columba made his pious landfall,
the purple, ankle-deep, hung like a mantle

on the starved shoulder of the moor.
Heather! I'd thought, the year I first
set foot, in Maine, among blueberries'

belled, pallid scurf; then—But there's
no heather *here*. Right to begin with:
botanically, they're all one family.

27

I saw that pallor, then, as an attenuation
in the west: the pioneers, the children's
children of the pioneers, look up from

the interior's plowed-under grassland,
the one homeland they know no homeland
but a taken-over turf: no sanction, no cover

but the raveled sleeve of empire: and yearn
for the pristine, the named, the fabulous,
the holy places. But from this island—

its nibbled turf, sheep trails, rabbit
droppings, harebells, mosses' brass-
starred, sodden firmament, the plink

of plover on that looped, perennial,
vast circumnavigation: at ground level
an incessant whimpering as everything,

however minuscule, joins the resistance
to the omnipresent wind—the prospect
is to the west. Here at the raw edge

of Europe—limpet tenacities, the tidal
combings, purplings of kelp and dulse,
the wrack, the blur, the breakup

of every prospect but turmoil, of
upheaval in the west—the retrospect
is once again toward the interior:

backward-looking, child of the child
of pioneers, forward-slogging with
their hooded caravels, their cattle,

and the fierce covered coal of doctrine
from what beleaguered hearth-fire of
the Name, they could not speculate,

such was the rigor of the Decalogue's
Thou Shalt Not—I now discover that
what looked, still looks, like revelation

was not hell-fire, no air-splintering
phosphorus of injunction, no Power,
no force whatever, but an opening

at the water's edge: a little lake,
world's eye, the mind's counterpart,
an eyeblink of reflection wrung from

the unreflecting seethe and chirr and
whimper of the prairie, the wind-
stirred grass, incognizant incognito

(all flesh being grass) of the mind's
resistance to the omnipresence of what
moves but has no, cannot say its name.

There at the brim of an illumination
that can't be entered, can't be lived in—
you'd either founder, a castaway, or drown—

a well, a source that comprehends, that
supersedes all doctrine: what surety,
what reprieve from drowning, is there,

other than in names? The prairie eyeblink,
stirred, grows murmurous—a murderous,
a monstrous world rimmed by the driftwood

of embarkations, landings, dooms, conquests,
missionary journeys, memorials: Columba
in the skin-covered wicker of that coracle,

lofting these stonily decrepit preaching
posts above the heathen purple; in their
chiseled gnarls, dimmed by the weatherings

of a millennium and more, the braided syntax
of a zeal ignited somewhere to the east,
concealed in hovels, quarreled over,

portaged westward: a basket weave, a
fishing net, a weir to catch, to salvage
some tenet, some common intimation for

all flesh, to hold on somehow till
the last millennium: as though the routes,
the ribbonings and redoublings, the

attenuations, spent supply lines, frayed-
out gradual of the retreat from empire, all
its castaways, might still bear witness.

I I

HABITATS

GRASSES

Undulant across the slopes
a gloss of purple
day by day arrives to dim
the green, as grasses

I never learned the names of—
numberless, prophetic,
transient—put on a flowering
so multiform, one

scarcely notices: the oats grow tall,
their pendent helmetfuls
of mica-drift, examined stem
by stem, disclose

alloys so various, enamelings
of a vermeil so
craftless, I all but despair of
ever reining in a

metaphor for: even the plebeian
dooryard plantain's
every homely cone-tip earns a
halo, a seraphic

hatband of guarantee that
dying, for
the unstudied, multitudinously,
truly lowly,

has no meaning, is nothing
if not flowering's
swarming reassurances of one
more resurrection.

ALDERS

The roadway's sallow, puddled furrow
uncurls like a root among the alders,
then flops up where the granite surfaces,
a bare outcrop. Alders are hard to stop—
impossible, even, unless you're really serious.

Someone who wasn't, from the look
of it, has done a little hacking at them
along the edges; but to deal with the alder—
the way it's dealt with down by the inlet—
means slash and burn, year by year by year.

It's not only the alders. Nothing's
the way it was. The jack pine's closing in—
a herd of brassy, burgeoning antlers
now bars the opening down to the shore.
Cut off, branch-stung, I find myself in tears

for all sorts of likely and unlikely reasons.
We try another way, between green-creamy
headlamps of mountain ash, wet peat moss
underfoot, dim elegiac voices of white-
throated sparrows above a dwindling trace

we halfway recognize, to a high ledge
where we once picnicked—a tight, finical
medallion that turns out to be a bench mark
setting its seal on the would-be primeval,
while everywhere the alders take the tundra back,

take back the fields and the four cellar holes
left by the settlers who made it their business,
come spring, to clear away the winter's frost-
heaved boulders, and to keep down the alders.
I'd once supposed these acres had no past—

that entity, no virgin, bled with the season,
burgeoned, withered, bloomed and bled again,
uninterfered with, like the pattern of a dance,
not the unarmed uprising of this
landlock, these tough true inhabitants.

BLUEBERRYING IN AUGUST

Sprung from the hummocks
of this island, stemmed,
sea-spray-fed chromosomes
trait-coded, say, for eyes
of that surprising blue
some have, that you have:
they're everywhere, these
mimic apertures the color
of distances, of drowning—

of creekside bluebells
islanded in the lost world
of childhood; of the
illusory indigo that moats
these hillocks when
the air is windless.

Today, though, there is
wind: a slate sag occludes
the afternoon with old,
hound-throated mutterings.
Offshore, the lighthouse
fades to a sheeted,
sightless ghost. August
grows somber. Though the blue-
eyed chromosome gives way,
living even so, minute to
minute, was never better.

THE BEACH PEA

FOR SUSAN RICH SHERIDAN

That first summer, what little
we'd learned of the geography
kept its own counsel—a vaporous
drip and sob, the whistle buoy
lowing offshore, the mittened
treacheries of ledge and tidefall,
mysteries of repose lapped and
delivered in a shawl of breakers.
Blundering through fog, late
one day, along an alder-bordered
track disclosed a meadow, at
its seaward edge a house,
its looming, boarded-up remoteness
big with soliloquy.
                A decade later
we skirted that same meadow, in
daisy-freckled sunshine, to find her
kerchiefed, statuesque
among the rocks—a collie
her one companion where
the beach pea flourished
untended, garish in the midst of
such concussion and dismemberment,
tide after tide, gale after gale; the house
behind her, its now unshuttered
solitudes delivered into daylight,
and back of that the larger
solitude of alder pockets, snarled
spruce, tamarack, pincushion
plush and calico of heath plants,

rockbottom footholds of the
purple iris, the sphagnum deeps,
small vivid orchids with
their feet in quicksand.
                Before her,
poised at the edge—the day
was one of bone-white splendor,
a slow surf filleting the blue—
lay a view such as one comes to
be at home with, to rest in,
intimate as with the hollows of
a lover's body: needled diadem
and fractured granite centered,
as in an altarpiece with kneeling
figures, on the inverted pendant
of 'Tit Manan light, its turning
gaze above the driftwood
phased like a moon.
                No sometime
visitor, by then, she'd come, drawn
by some such perception (she herself
was never so explicit) to live here;
come in fact—though we'd not, from
any hint of hers, have guessed—
to die here.
              The weight of an
adieu, each summer, overhangs
the solstice—the weightier,
the more immaculate the daylight's
interfusing blue. Some throb
of sorrow, of the apprehended
and consented to, reproved
our quashed tiff (we'd been bickering,
the two of us, for days) the day
we saw her last, that summer,

that serene, last,
perfect afternoon.
                    Word came
in January: she might just possibly
live through the spring. Midsummer,
that year, found us in Northumberland:
white midnights, gray days
of drizzle, the laburnum's
golden dross on all the sidewalks—
kin of broom and gorse, of
the acacia, the beach pea . . .
The beach pea! That, in retrospect,
was the connection: tough,
ubiquitous, perennial, intimate
of granite and driftwood, of all
those ponderous displacements
at the edge: so unaspiring,
so mundane, except—
except for, looked at
up close, those tendrils,
those reaching rings
that now encircle nothing.

HIGH NOON

The poplars gray as a ghost by the creek,
fiddlehead coils still in fuzz, the spruces
tipped fingerling green, tamaracks gauzing
the bog, the aspens translucent, a tremor
      lit from within—oh, and the air

here, the sea air an easterly rinsing
of appletrees so decrepit, so crabbed
at the knuckle, it's a wonder they manage
to keep it up, year after year, though
      the fragrance is ageless:

carmine love-knots unclenching to a rose-
pink pucker that whitens as it breaks open,
admitting the offices of pollen-combing, nectar-
siphoning bees: all these, at the beginning
      of June, one could count on,

could even halfway ignore, as one tends to
ignore the ubiquitous roadside spindrift
of the cinquefoil—spreading, prodigal,
threadily elaborate rehearsal in minuscule
      of the roses to follow:

all this is dependable, companionable even,
in its way, as the weather is—the gales
and the fog, if you're not a fisherman. What
we've tended, cravenly, to shy away from is
      the dolor of the particular:

who's not speaking to whom, who's ailing
and doesn't get out any more, who's still
around and who's not. We've seen Lorna
out weeding her dahlia bed, we've noted
          her tough old tomcat

snoozing as usual at the door of her trailer,
and though she complains that with her back
and all she's not good for much, she seems
cheerful as ever. It's about Amanda
          we keep putting off inquiring

as the days pass, and the poplars are out
of their dim natal down, the shade's
a deckled gallery of ferns, the woodwind
tremolo of the first of June is subsumed
          by the monotone of midsummer,

and while the cinquefoil blooms and blooms
as though time had no meaning, and
the last limp tatters have frayed from
the appletrees, and in the air, here and there,
          the smell of roses is already

voluptuous, one day we meet her, out walking:
still light of foot as a girl, not a thread
of white in the nest under the hairnet, though
it's thirteen years since Ned died, and
          she still wakes up screeching

sometimes in the night, it's so lonesome
there in that childless, scrubbed, painfully
immaculate house; and the sidelong indigo
of her look—what an incorrigible flirt she
          still is!—has closed down now

to a pinpoint, she can't see to piece together
another quilt block, embroider a pillowcase, or
do wildflower watercolors the way she used to; but
she hasn't ceased to keep track of what's opening
      by the roadsides; just yesterday,

she tells us, she went over to the neighbors'
with a bouquet in her hand, announcing,
"What this house needs is pink roses!"
Down by the shore, where we are, there are
      masses of *Rosa rugosa,*

which thanks to some spin of the chromosomes,
instead of the gaudy usual quasi-magenta
come out (with just the slightest
hint of a blush in the bud beforehand)
      moon-white at high noon,

and strange. In a blown-up photograph she
once showed us, it's that time of day, she's
gone down to the beach with a girlfriend,
and there she is, laughing, unmistakably
      ravishing, in that welter

of foliage and thorns and silk uncrumpling,
moon-white at high noon, as though when the sun
leaves the zenith (if it ever does) of that
monochrome, it will utter its frivolous last
      gasp in a smother of roses.

A WHIPPOORWILL IN THE WOODS

Night after night, it was very nearly enough,
they said, to drive you crazy: a whippoorwill
in the woods repeating itself like the stuck groove
of an LP with a defect, and no way possible
of turning the thing off.

And night after night, they said, in the insomniac
small hours the whipsawing voice of obsession
would have come in closer, the way a sick
thing does when it's done for—or maybe the reason
was nothing more melodramatic

than a night-flying congregation of moths, lured in
in their turn by house-glow, the strange heat
of it—imagine the nebular dangerousness, if one
were a moth, the dark pockmarked with beaks, the great
dim shapes, the bright extinction—

if moths are indeed, after all, what a whippoorwill
favors. Who knows? Anyhow, from one point of view
insects are to be seen as an ailment, moths above all:
the filmed-over, innumerable nodes of spun-out tissue
untidying the trees, the larval

spew of such hairy hordes, one wonders what use
they can be other than as a guarantee no bird
goes hungry. We're like that. The webbiness,
the gregariousness of the many are what we can't abide.
We single out for notice

above all what's disjunct, the way birds are,
with their unhooked-up, cheekily anarchic
dartings and flashings, their uncalled-for color—
the indelible look of the rose-breasted grosbeak
          an aunt of mine, a noticer

of such things before the noticing had or needed
a name, drew my five-year-old attention up to, in
the green deeps of a maple. She never married,
believed her cat had learned to leave birds alone,
          and for years, node after node,

by lingering degrees she made way within for
what wasn't so much a thing as it was a system,
a webwork of error that throve until it killed her.
What is health? We must all die sometime.
          Whatever it is, out there

in the woods, that begins to seem like
a species of madness, we survive as we can:
the hooked-up, the humdrum, the brief, tragic
wonder of being at all. The whippoorwill out in
          the woods, for me, brought back

as by a relay, from a place at such a distance
no recollection now in place could reach so far,
the memory of a memory she told me of once:
of how her father, my grandfather, by whatever
          now unfathomable happenstance,

carried her (she might have been five) into the breathing night.
"Listen!" she said he'd said. "Did you hear it?
That was a whippoorwill." And she (and I) never forgot.

A WINTER BURIAL

From tall rooms, largesse of peonies,
the porches summercool, the bed upstairs
immaculate in its white counterpane,

to kerosene-lit evenings, the wind
an orphan roaming the silver maples,
sudden widowhood: to meaner comforts,

a trumpetvine above the kitchen door,
then one night her new husband didn't
come in from the milking: to the lot

she bought with what that place went
for, dwindlings in a doll's house: to
the high-rise efficiency condominium,

television on all day, to the cubicle
in the denominational home, to total
unprivacy of bed and bedpan, nurse shoes,

TV with no picture or else coming in waves,
a vertigo: to, one nightfall when the last
weak string gave way that had held whatever

she was, that mystery, together, the bier
that waited—there were no planes coming in,
not many made it to the funeral, the blizzard

had been so bad, the graveyard drifted
so deep, so many severed limbs of trees
thrown down, they couldn't get in to plow

an opening for the hearse, or shovel
the cold white counterpane from that cell
in the hibernal cupboard, till the day after.

PORTOLA VALLEY

A dense ravine, no inch
of which was level until
some architect niched in this
shimmer of partition, fishpond
and flowerbed, these fording-
stones' unwalled steep staircase
down to where (speak softly) you
take off your shoes, step onto
guest-house tatami matting,
learn to be Japanese.

There will be red wine,
artichokes, and California
politics for dinner; a mockingbird may whisper, a frog rasp
and go kerplunk, the shifting
inlay of goldfish in the court-
yard floor add to your vertigo;
and deer look in, the velvet
thrust of pansy faces and vast
violet-petal ears, inquiring,
stun you without a blow.

A MINOR TREMOR

Lunch hour in flowery,
eucalypt-boled Berkeley:
a spume off the Pacific
just scathed the easy-going sun
as equilibrium
on surreptitious horseback

bucked, dipped, swung
like a censer. A minor
tremor, said the habitué.
I looked about me
with no alarm.
We had been talking

of Milton, I remember.
The oracles are dumb;
with hollow shriek the steep
(he wrote) *of Delphos leaving.*
Not so. The unbroken broncoes
of Horse Poseidon

are the least of it. Moloch
is back, a still bigger spender.
Frenzy's a drugstore commodity.
The lost sheep feast daily
on the scaly horror
with Perrier and french fries.

SAVANNAH

FOR BEE CLOSE LANE

Not quite diaphanous, not Spanish,
not a moss, weft after weft
depends from chambered
rafterings of liveoak,
green square leading
to green square, from
opening to opening, as
in a courtship—at whose
discovered center leaps
this rose-leaf
relinquishment,
this falling.
              Yes.
To fall. To ripen
and then wither.
That is all.
              Oh, not all
at all. The bed-curtained,
quickening and ripening
dream of the body,
of fair women, torn
by an obelisk
to the Confederate dead:
the ramparts breached,
the powder magazine's
uproar, the maimed,
sullen giving way,
inform these
mansionings.

A stillness
out there, past thicketings
of juniper, bullbrier
and yaupon, flailed
thrashings of palmetto,
out past the hiss
of cordgrass:
enveloping
the drop-sleeve
creak of shrimp boats,
a dim, large,
smothering,
incessant
shrug.

AMHERST

May 15, 1987

The oriole, a charred and singing coal,
still burns aloud among the monuments,
its bugle call to singularity the same
unheard (she wrote) as to the crowd,
this graveyard gathering, the audience
        she never had.

Fame has its own dynamic, its smolderings
and ignitions, its necessary distance:
Colonel Higginson, who'd braved the cannon,
admitted his relief not to live near such
breathless, hushed excess (you cannot
        fold a flood,

she wrote, and put it in a drawer), such
stoppered prodigies, compressions and
devastations within the atom—*all this
world contains: his face*—the civil
wars of just one stanza. A universe
        might still applaud,

the red at bases of the trees (she wrote)
like mighty footlights burn, God still
look on, his badge a raised hyperbole—
inspector general of all that carnage,
those gulfs, those fleets and crews
        of solid blood:

the battle fought between the soul and No
One There, no one at all, where cities
ooze away: unbroken prairies of air
without a settlement. On Main Street
the hemlock hedge grows up untrimmed,
          the light that poured

in once like judgment (whether it was noon
at night, or only heaven at noon, she wrote,
she could not tell) cut off, the wistful,
the merely curious, in her hanging dress discern
an ikon; her ambiguities are made a shrine,
          then violated;

we've drunk champagne above her grave, declaimed
the lines of one who dared not live aloud.
I thought of writing her (Dear Emily, though,
seems too intrusive, Dear Miss Dickinson too prim)
to ask, not without irony, what, wherever she
          is now, is made

of all the racket, whether she's of two minds
still; and tell her how on one cleared hillside,
an ample peace that looks toward Norwottuck's
unaltered purple has been shaken since
by bloodshed on Iwo Jima, in Leyte Gulf
          and Belleau Wood.

THE HURRICANE AND
CHARLOTTE MEW

The trees are down all over the south of England—
   the green, tossed
tops of beeches and sycamores in the deer park at Knole,
the Sussex oaks, the clumped pine-tufts in what had been
   left of Ashdown Forest,
upended by the winds of a hurricane hurled in,
improbably, all the way from the Caribbean, on the
   heels of what began
   as an ordinary rain

like the fine gray rain she remembered had been falling
   the day the last
roped bole at the end of Euston Square Gardens, after
a week's work of sawing, dismembering, and carting off,
   gave way and fell,
and what gave way within her, for what was gone, had
a finality that, for her, was apocalyptic, but was also
   no more tangible
   a wisp than the handful

she'd seen the shade-catchers, sister and brother, snatch
   as they ran past.
But that would have been while the great tossed tops at
   the end of the garden
stood, as they were standing all over the south of England
until that night, surprised by some flaw in the flow of the
   Gulf Stream, they fell
by the thousand, the tens of thousands. Ashdown Forest will not
   be the same again.

What persists, what is not to be uprooted or dismembered,
        I would discover,
sauntering there with a girl and a boy with a kite, last year,
        is the vast,
skittish, shade-catching turmoil of more usual English weather—
        the wet, head-high bracken,
the drippingly black-and-gold gorse we sheltered under.
Notwithstanding the great, stunned, fallen stems that lie there,
Charlotte Mew, had she been with us, would have been
        part of the fun.

DEJECTION: A FOOTNOTE

Out of a bow-windowed, mingy, doleful
little room at Keswick—August throngs
moiling wet cobblestones—I fled
offended into worsening weather,

wrapped in a flapping gale's
extravagance, the vestment of an id
that's not at home, that finds no comfort
other than in visions of disaster,

fire, famine, slaughter, shipwreck:
it's there in all of us, as Coleridge knew,
invoking for a surrogate this flailing
at the shores of Derwentwater:

had known since, eight years old,
he fled the prospect of a whipping
he admittedly deserved to some
degree, to hide down by the river,

thinking (half of Ottery St. Mary
out looking for him all night long),
with horrid relish, what misery all
this misery must cause his mother.

Calves stood bawling in the field;
the weather worsened; ponds were dragged;
at dawn he was discovered, rigid, and
borne home. Two decades later,

here in the shadow of the same Skiddaw
(I watch from an unheated loo the vapors
dragged along its glum green velvet
like an udder or a trawl, and hear

that same surrogate, still screaming
worse than a blizzard or a fiend,
as though the date weren't August
but the middle of the winter)

at some recollecting noise, he
found the scene exactly as he'd left it:
the bawling calf, the howling infant,
the self a willful, a total stranger.

EASEDALE TARN

Annuities of peat moss,
sedge, bog cotton, bracken
to be trekked through

halfway up the beck's hung
watershed, today still
unwalled common, where

a sheep, though owned
and earmarked, may
still go astray, may

utter its little cry, or,
suddenly aware of where
it's come to—this crag,

this waterfall, this rosebush
arched and glittering
beside it—freeze,

feel the earth's forward
motion, its hurtling,
harrowing retrograde:

past farmsteads, through
gated openings they,
Dorothy and William,

must also, repeatedly,
have passed through,
bound for the source

of all the babble
down there among the
hollies and the hazels—

the mountain basin
still withheld from
view, though to the

inland-moving gulls
that hang above it
it's in no way secret,

nor is it to these
vaporous tributaries,
nor to the air that's

everywhere the habitat
of rising to just such
occasions as the twain

who once inhaled it, in
this very place, may be
said to have invented—

primeval cisterns'
tremor, the blazing
drumskin of rain.

FIREWEED

A single seedling, camp-follower
of arson—frothing bombed-out
rubble with rose-purple lotfuls

unwittingly as water overbrims,
tarn-dark or sun-ignited, down
churnmilk rockfalls—aspiring

from the foothold of a London
roof-ledge, taken wistful note of
by an uprooted prairie-dweller,

less settled in St. Martin's Lane
(no lane now but a riverbed of
noise) than even the unlikely

blackbird that's to be heard here,
gilding and regilding a matutinal
ancestral scripture, unwitting

of past devastation as of what
remains: spires, finials, lofted
domes, the homiletic caveat

underneath—*Here wee have no
continuing citty*—by the Dean
whose effigy survived one burning.

III

A SORT OF FOOTHOLD

VACANT LOT WITH POKEWEED

Tufts, follicles, grubstake
biennial rosettes, a low-
life beach-blond scruff of
couch grass: notwithstanding
the interglinting dregs

of wholesale upheaval and
dismemberment, weeds do not
hesitate, the wheeling
rise of the ailanthus halts
at nothing—and look! here's

a pokeweed, sprung from seed
dropped by some vagrant, that's
seized a foothold: a magenta-
girdered bower, gazebo twirls
of blossom rounding into

raw-buttoned, garnet-rodded
fruit one more wayfarer
perhaps may salvage from
the season's frittering,
the annual wreckage.

THE SUBWAY SINGER

Survivor and unwitting
public figure—a gaunter one
since with her cane, accordion
and cup, I last saw her

tap her hard way along
the hurled col, with its serial
crevasses, of an IRT train,
and heard the cracked bell

of her battered alto rung
again above the grope and jostle,
the knee-jerk compunction
of the herd at the faint signal

it's all but past hearing,
from beyond the ashen
headland, the mist-shrouded
hollows of her lifted

sightlessness—seen waiting
now on the platform, as it were
between appearances, a public figure
shrunken but still recognizable,

she links in one unwitting
community how many who have heard
and re-heard that offering's fall
toward the poorbox of oblivion?

MY COUSIN MURIEL

From Manhattan, a glittering shambles
of enthrallments and futilities, of leapers
in leotards, scissoring vortices blurred,
this spring evening, by the *punto in aria*
of hybrid pear trees in bloom (no troublesome
fruit to follow) my own eyes are drawn to—
childless spinner of metaphor, in touch
by way of switchboard and satellite, for
the last time ever, with my cousin Muriel:

mother of four, worn down by arthritis,
her kidneys wasting, alone in a hospital
somewhere in California: in that worn voice,
the redhead's sassy timbre eroded from it,
while the unspeakable stirs like a stone,
a strange half-absence and a tone of weakness
(Wordsworth's discharged soldier comes to mind)
as she inquires, fatigued past irony, "How's
your work going?" As for what was hers—

nursing-home steam-table clamor, scummed
soup fat, scrubbed tubers, bones, knives,
viscera, cooking odors lived with till
they live with you, a settlement in the
olfactory tissue—well, it's my function
to imagine scenes, try for connections
as I'm trying now: a grope for words,
the numb, all but immobilized trajectory
to where my cousin, whom I've seen just once

since she went there to live, lies dying:
part of the long-drawn larger movement
that lured the Reverend Charles Wadsworth
to San Francisco, followed in imagination
from the cupola of the shuttered homestead
in Amherst where a childless recluse,
on a spring evening a century ago, A.D.
(so to speak) 1886, would cease to breathe
the air of rural Protestant New England—

an atmosphere and a condition which
by stages, wagon trains, tent meetings,
the Revival, infused the hinterland
my cousin Muriel and I both hailed from:
a farmhouse childhood, kerosene-lit,
tatting-and-mahogany genteel. "You
were the smart one," she'd later say.
Arrant I no doubt was; as for imagining
scenes, it must be she'd forgotten

the melodramas she once improvised above
the dolls' tea-table: "For the pity's sake!
How could you get us all in such a fix?
Well, I s'pose we'll just have to make
the best of it"—the whole trajectory of
being female, while I played the dullard,
presaged. She bloomed, knew how to flirt,
acquired admirers. I didn't. In what I now
recall as a last teen-age heart-to-heart,

I'm saying I don't plan on getting married.
"Not ever?" "Not ever"—then, craven, "Oh,
I'd like to be *engaged*." Which is what she
would have been, by then, to Dorwin Voss,
whom I'd been sweet on in fifth grade (last

painless crush before the crash of puberty)—
blue-eyed, black-haired, good-looking Dorwin,
who'd later walk out on her and their kids,
moving on again, part of the larger exodus

from the evangel-haunted prairie hinterland.
Some stayed; the more intemperate of us
headed east—a Village basement, uptown
lunch hours, vertiginous delusions of
autonomy, the bar crowd; waiting for
some well-heeled dullard of a male to
deign to phone, or for a stumbling-
drunk, two-timing spouse's key to turn
the small-hour dark into another fracas—

others for California: the lettuce fields,
Knott's Berry Farm, the studios; palms,
slums, sprinklers, canyon landslides,
fuchsia hedges hung with hummingbirds,
the condominium's kempt squalor: whatever
Charles Wadsworth, out there, foresaw
as consolation for anyone at all—attached,
estranged, or merely marking time—little
is left, these days, these times, to say

when the unspeakable stirs like a stone.
Pulled threads, the shared fabric of a
summer memory: the state fair campground,
pump water, morning light through tent flaps,
the promenade among the booths: blue-ribbon
zinnias and baby beeves, the cooled marvel
of a cow, life size, carved out of butter;
a gypsy congeries without a shadow on it
but the domed torpor of the capitol

balalooning, ill at ease, egregious
souvenir of pomp among the cornfields;
kewpie-doll lowlife along the midway,
the bleachers after dark where, sick
with mirth, under the wanton stars,
for the ineptitude of clowns, we soared
in arabesques of phosphorus, and saw—
O dread and wonder, O initiating taste
of ecstasy—a man shot from a cannon.

Too young then to know how much we knew
already of experience, how little of
its wider paradigm, enthralled by that
punto in aria of sheer excitement, we who
are neither leaf nor bole—O hybrid
pear tree, cloned fruitless blossomer!—
suspend, uprooted from the hinterland,
this last gray filament across a continent
where the unspeakable stirs like a stone.

A HEDGE OF RUBBER TREES

The West Village by then was changing; before long
the rundown brownstones at its farthest edge
would have slipped into trendier hands. She lived,
impervious to trends, behind a potted hedge of
rubber trees, with three cats, a canary—refuse
from whose cage kept sifting down and then
germinating, a yearning seedling choir, around
the saucers on the windowsill—and an inexorable
cohort of roaches she was too nearsighted to deal
with, though she knew they were there, and would
speak of them, ruefully, as of an affliction that
     might once, long ago, have been prevented.

Unclassifiable castoffs, misfits, marginal cases:
when you're one yourself, or close to it, there's
a reassurance in proving you haven't quite gone
under by taking up with somebody odder than you are.
Or trying to. "They're my *friends*," she'd say of
her cats—Mollie, Mitzi and Caroline, their names were,
and she was forever taking one or another in a cab
to the vet—as though she had no others. The roommate
who'd become a nun, the one who was Jewish, the couple
she'd met on a foliage tour, one fall, were all people
she no longer saw. She worked for a law firm, said all
     the judges were alcoholic, had never voted.

But would sometimes have me to dinner—breaded veal,
white wine, strawberry Bavarian—and sometimes, from
what she didn't know she was saying, I'd snatch a shred
or two of her threadbare history. Baltic cold. Being

sent home in a troika when her feet went numb. In
summer, carriage rides. A swarm of gypsy children
driven off with whips. An octogenarian father, bishop
of a dying schismatic sect. A very young mother
who didn't want her. A half-brother she met just once.
Cousins in Wisconsin, one of whom phoned her from a candy
store, out of the blue, while she was living in Chicago.
    What had brought her there, or when, remained unclear.

As did much else. We'd met in church. I noticed first
a big, soaring soprano with a wobble in it, then
the thickly wreathed and braided crimp in the mouse-
gold coiffure. Old? Young? She was of no age.
Through rimless lenses she looked out of a child's,
or a doll's, globular blue. Wore Keds the year round,
tended otherwise to overdress. Owned a mandolin. Once
I got her to take it down from the mantel and plink out,
through a warm fuddle of sauterne, a lot of giddy Italian
airs from a songbook whose pages had started to crumble.
The canary fluffed and quivered, and the cats, amazed,
    came out from under the couch and stared.

What could the offspring of schismatic age and a
reluctant child bride expect from life? Not much.
Less and less. A dream she'd had kept coming back,
years after. She'd taken a job in Washington with
some right-wing lobby, and lived in one of those
bow-windowed mansions that turn into roominghouses,
and her room there had a full-length mirror: oval,
with a molding, is the way I picture it. In her dream
something woke her, she got up to look, and there
in the glass she saw she had no face, or whatever
face she'd had was covered over—she gave it
    a wondering emphasis—with gray veils.

The West Village was changing. I was changing. The last
time I asked her to dinner, she didn't show. Hours—
or was it days?—later, she phoned to explain: she hadn't
been able to find my block; a patrolman had steered her home.
I spent my evenings canvassing for Gene McCarthy. Passing,
I'd see her shades drawn, no light behind the rubber trees.
She wasn't out, she didn't own a TV. She was in there,
getting gently blotto. What came next, I wasn't brave
enough to want to know. Only one day, passing, I saw
new shades, quick-chic matchstick bamboo, going up where
the waterstained old ones had been, and where the seedlings—
O gray veils, gray veils—had risen and gone down.

THE HALLOWEEN PARADE

Rollicking into Bleecker Street
with the maskers, the sashaying
effigies jointed like mantises
or a cornfield come to town, a rube's
    Birnam-to-Dunsinane,

had been more than fun, had been
akin to a levitation, such as
Isabel Archer of Albany, say, may be
said to have traveled to Rome for—
    or anyhow a speeded-up

latterday travesty of it: to be
swept away, caught up in a spate
of appearances, gorgeous, gorgonish,
déraciné—O saturnalian
    anonymity of cities!

Let it be said: though our grandeurs
were tacky, at least we were honest:
what we looked for was no more
than a license to be silly
    about what matters,

or did once, or was supposed to:
all those tessellated acres
under the dome, the soaring
interior spaces Isabel still
    found it possible

to imagine a meaning for, far
from what, in the hinterland,
would already have been happening:
statehouse domes going up like
      a crop of mushrooms,

gilt and marble for schoolchildren
to be herded under, heel plates
skittering; a hireling amplitude,
its meaning gone: what's there
      to admire but speed,

what's left to look up to but a
rocket-thrust, a sitcom celebrity?
This being what all the rush
of westward-the-course-of-empire
      finally comes down to:

to be free, as Isabel Archer pig-
headedly put it, to meet one's fate,
to take one's chances, try on
disguises, the Dies Irae synco-
      pating to Bye, Bye

Blackbird, How Dry I Am—
to meet the Day of Doom
on roller skates, as every
other masker, that year,
      seemed to be doing:

and I wonder now—having heard
piecemeal what became of him,
as I learned how he'd slipped
and fractured an elbow, roller-
      skating—was he there

73

too, rollicking into Bleecker Street,
having more than fun, upborne
among the effigies—O prodigious
anonymities of Manhattan!—his manner
    more than ever outré,

as the dwindling of the very memory
of manners tends on occasion to
beget a great deal of Manner—
who was to linger in the oxygen
    tent of his fate

for weeks before it claimed him,
one of many and therefore exemplary?
O reedbed Dunsinane of the undone,
of chances taken! To be free to
    throw one's life away

as Isabel Archer, alone in the
dimmed drawing room of her fate,
would know she had done: O how many
have sat like this: a window ledge
    above the lava flow,

the ice floe, the interminable
howling off the Hudson! There was
the student from some other country
who one night slipped out of her room
    to mail a letter

and was not seen again until,
months later, miles upriver, tidal
currents washed whatever had been
left of her ashore. Otherwise,
    only rumors. That was all

a long, long time ago: out of the
rivering anonymity of cities,
the tidal froth of choices
made, the flotsam of All
    Hallows, washed ashore.

NOTHING STAYS PUT

IN MEMORY OF FATHER FLYE, 1884–1985

The strange and wonderful are too much with us.
The protea of the antipodes—a great,
globed, blazing honeybee of a bloom—
for sale in the supermarket! We are in
our decadence, we are not entitled.
What have we done to deserve
all the produce of the tropics—
this fiery trove, the largesse of it
heaped up like cannonballs, these pineapples, bossed
and crested, standing like troops at attention,
these tiers, these balconies of green, festoons
grown sumptuous with stoop labor?

The exotic is everywhere, it comes to us
before there is a yen or a need for it. The green-
grocers, uptown and down, are from South Korea.
Orchids, opulence by the pailful, just slightly
fatigued by the plane trip from Hawaii, are
disposed on the sidewalks; alstroemerias, freesias
fattened a bit in translation from overseas; gladioli
likewise estranged from their piercing ancestral crimson;
as well as, less altered from the original blue cornflower
of the roadsides and railway embankments of Europe, these
bachelor's buttons. But it isn't the railway embankments
their featherweight wheels of cobalt remind me of, it's

a row of them among prim colonnades of cosmos,
snapdragon, nasturtium, bloodsilk red poppies,
in my grandmother's garden: a prairie childhood,
the grassland shorn, overlaid with a grid,

unsealed, furrowed, harrowed and sown with immigrant grasses,
their massive corduroy, their wavering feltings embroidered
here and there by the scarlet shoulder patch of cannas
on a courthouse lawn, by a love knot, a cross stitch
of living matter, sown and tended by women,
nurturers everywhere of the strange and wonderful,
beneath whose hands what had been alien begins,
as it alters, to grow as though it were indigenous.

But at this remove what I think of as
strange and wonderful, strolling the side streets of Manhattan
on an April afternoon, seeing hybrid pear trees in blossom,
a tossing, vertiginous colonnade of foam, up above—
is the white petalfall, the warm snowdrift
of the indigenous wild plum of my childhood.
Nothing stays put. The world is a wheel.
All that we know, that we're
made of, is motion.

I V

THE PRAIRIE

THE PRAIRIE

I

The wind whines in the elevator shaft. The houseless
squinny at us, mumbling. We walk attuned
to the colubrine rustle of a proletariat

that owes nobody anything, through a Manhattan
otherwise (George Eliot's phrase) well wadded
in stupidity—a warren of unruth, a propped

vacuity: our every pittance under lock and key
a party to the general malfeasance. Saurian,
steam-wreathed rancors crowd the manholes,

as though somebody grappled with the city's
entrails: Laocoön, doomsayer, by a god
or gods undone. Whom nobody believed, of course.

No, better, as the muse of what's become
of us, invoke Chekhov's imagined Jew who put—
out of demented principle—the rubles he'd

inherited into the stove. Money-burning:
however jaded you may think you are, now there's
a scandal for you. Six thousand rubles,

and he burns them: shows no respect, fears
no one, is a man possessed, the evil sprite
out of a nightmare: thus Chekhov, scandal-

mongering. Grandson of a serf, son of a
storekeeper, brought up to the chink of kopecks
at Taganrog: spring mud and summer dust,

burdocks, beatings, piety. Money and profits:
the mainspring for all of us, except that brother
of a tavernkeeping Jew, who mocks us,

boasting he put his money in the stove.
So Chekhov tells us—who, half a nomad,
consorted with the nomads of Sakhalin—yurt-

dwellers who never washed, who planted nothing,
saw the plow as a transgression; whose numbers
were already in decline; who smelled, up close,

as all unbathed and houseless wanderers do,
of sweat, soil, urine: living nit-encrusted,
matted, shivering. One forgets, here in

half-stupefied Manhattan, how much of everything
that happens happens (Simone Weil's relentless
phrase) far from hot baths. The wind howls

from across the Hudson: lost, lost. Marx
and Engels, Lenin, Red October: since Chekhov
(no ideologue) wrote of the general malfeasance

"We do not care, it does not interest us,"
however much has changed, still nothing changes.
Demagoguery. Boundaries. Forced marches.

Monoculture on the heels of slash and burn.
Land reform. Drought. Insects. Drainage.
Long-term notes. Collectives. Tractor lugs.

Names: brunizem and chernozem; culm,
rhizome and stolon. A fibrous, root-fattened
hinterland of grass. The steppe. The prairie.

A chance fact leaps into place: that Anton Chekhov
came howling (as only the stillborn can
fail to do) into existence at Taganrog

the year my father's father, no doubt howling
too, endured the shock of entry. Add the link
of early memory: the prairie, the steppe—

a shimmering caul of namelessness, of voices,
unauthenticated, multitudinous, in wait
for (so Chekhov wrote) a muse, a scribe, a bard.

2

The year is 1860. February. Still hard winter.
A cabin of hewn logs, on sixty acres
of raw grassland, prairie yet unturned.

One bed. Snow sifts through roof chinks.
Some nights the kettle freezes on the stove.
My great-grandfather gets what rest he can

on a quilt-covered pile of straw. A settler
from Indiana, his mind scarred by whippings;
a smattering of schooling, an appetite for land.

A hinterland of grass: tough, fertile,
root-nurtured chernozem ("black earth"
in Russian), nameless hitherto: lush midriff

of an empire Napoleon, having retaken it
from Spain (who didn't exactly own it) was now
hard pressed to trade for cash: bought in a hurry,

unlooked-at, for four cents an acre, by envoys
who'd exceeded their instructions, but who knew
what was imperative: land so rich, the more-

than-man-high panicles so dense, the nomad
aborigines for centuries had shunned it. Treaties
and forced marches brought them to it—treaties

made by chiefs who knew no better. Boundaries
were drawn; section by quarter section
platted, parceled, sold, speculated on,

built on; torn open, for the first time ever,
by plowshares—shouldering a dimming memory
of what had been, would never be again, aside.

A dimming memory of campsites: skin cones
smoke-stained, the base aglow, the moving shadow
of the life within revealed: two half circles

ranged about the sacred tree-bole, gift of
Wakonda, shining summoner of thunderbirds from
their imagined corners. A dimming memory of how,

toward the ending of the Moon When Nothing Happens,
spring thunder and the early-morning trilling
of meadowlarks returned, among the sloughs

the whooping cranes moved in again to dance
before they coupled—carmine-faced up close,
like painted women—and on higher ground

big-wattled prairie chickens thudded, courting.
All long gone. My father's father, as a boy
prone to anxieties, night terrors, straying

sometimes at dusk in unfenced spaces where
bell-clappered cattle roamed, had seen them—grand,
pagan, dreadful as the tree-bole of Ashtoreth.

The white man does not understand America,
a red man wrote: *the roots of the tree of his life
have yet to grasp it.* A dwindling memory

among the Omaha, a woodland people once,
whose remnant, up close, smell of the usual
sweat, soil, urine, vomit: a way of living lost.

Hard work. The settlers put a beleaguered foot down
against the shiftless, as their forebears had
concerning maypoles and the sanctus bell. Hard

work. Drainage ditches. Fences to keep in
the cattle. Now and then a grown man, entoiled
by evangelical dismay, would cry, "Lost! Lost!"

3

A nerve storm, a lapse or lesion, a blizzard
in the brain: at sixteen, grown up bookish,
hesitant, susceptible, my father's father

would blurt—his little sister looking up aghast,
the half-cleared supper table a bleak witness—
something about being done for, damned to hell—

something like that; to find, almost before his mother,
always the quicker one, could speak, the revulsion
gone; elation following, an astonished lightness.

What did it mean? He was never sure. A brimstone
rhetoric imbibed? A flareup—something in the glands,
like acne? He'd put it, at all events, behind him.

At twenty, wary of certitude, he shared questions,
and a bed, with one best friend. Nights, they
read Emerson together; after the swimming wick

went under, they'd go on talking. What was it
kept him so often wakeful, awed, while
the friend slept—what plank in reason, laid

unbroken, precarious, across the slough
of namelessness, its chucklings, its slitherings,
its shrieks, its spearheaded leaps and lunges?

Egorooshka, Chekhov's child-deputy, cocooned
among the wool bales, crossing the steppe,
heard the uneasy buzz and stir, the turmoil

when the wind rose. *An inlet into the deeps*
of Reason, Emerson had written: *out of*
unhandseled savage nature, out of the terrible

Druids and Berserkirs . . . We have listened too long
to the courtly muses. In self-trust all the virtues
are comprehended. . . . Self-trust. Man Thinking.

When—my father's father might have wondered—
was Man Thinking, self-reliant, other than
alone in the vast stammer of the inarticulate?

An absence. Creeks and timber. Wild plum, crabapple,
sumac along the fencerows. Tilled acres. Section lines.
Farmsteads that clot the vacancy, that cannot fill it—

the sense of exile, of something wrong: a dim
compunction finds Man Thinking anxious, as
all animals are anxious. In heath, duneland,

savanna, all treeless spaces, the immersing
sense of waiting, the unfathomable lassitude,
the purling, the quick tenuity of things.

The dead, wrote Emerson, aged twenty-two, *sleep*
in their moonless night. All history is an epitaph.
A few days more, and idle eyes will run

over your obituary, the world forget you.
The tenuity of being: Chekhov, who'd later
become a doctor, down with a fever, crossing

the steppe, tended by that innkeeping Jew.
My father's father ill with typhoid in a
Dakota roominghouse, a jolting two-day train ride

away from home. In that region of wind he'd bought,
with borrowed money, a treeless piece of land.
Back here, he'd met a girl—small, sprightly, husky-

voiced—who promised, when he headed north again,
to write. He found the homesteaders burning hay
for fuel. The season was wet and cold, the wind unending.

By midsummer he'd turned, with team and plow,
the sod of eighty hitherto uncultivated acres.
He took his bride there on their honeymoon.

4

We have listened too long to the courtly muses.
Perhaps. My father's father, from the spring
he turned the sod out there, preserved a sonnet:

There crowd my mind (he wrote) *vague fancies*
of Aeolian harpings, twined with weird oaks'
murmurings. In those wind-scathed solitudes,

impelled by absence so immense it all but
unpropped Man Thinking, he'd reached for that
old lore for reassurance—as one day a grandchild,

likewise impelled, would travel eastward,
backward to the precincts of grass-overrun,
mere, actual Dodona. A venture he'd

have been bemused by. I feel a halfway need
to justify, to whisper, Please don't disapprove,
don't think me frivolous. Can the courtly muses

of Europe, those bedizened crones, survive
the manholes, the vaunt and skitter of Manhattan, or
consort with the dug-in, the hunkering guardians

of the Dakotas? The Louisiana Purchase
passing (as it were) from hand to hand,
my father's father, having staked a claim

by planting trees there, rented out the eighty,
trekked back with his bride, a homing pair,
to set up as a storekeeper's son-in-law.

The year is 1885. Next spring will see a son
delivered yelling into the rooms above the store.
Still nobody is settled. The railroad

has made people restless. Chekhov too: in 1887,
bound from Moscow to Taganrog, he'd cross
the steppe again, this time by rail; would see

the wheelbarrows, the dugouts where the work crews
lived, mounded under the moon. By spring
of that same year, a railborne exodus

to California, the latest Land of Promise,
of figs and pomegranates, had begun. Whole
neighborhoods were going. In September

my grandparents-to-be would be among them.
From an uncushioned sleeping car, the first
arid glimpse of Colorado. The Spanish Peaks.

A washout in New Mexico. Immoderate heat
and chill. The desert's rigors and mirages.
Then Pasadena. Date palms. Dust. Ramshackle

houses. Gamblers. The bare arroyo. The mountain
wall. Pregnant again, my father's mother
had been trainsick all the way. Pasadena:

the name a borrowing from the Chippewa, who'd
never lived there. Of those who did, what history
there is is an erasure. Called—after the mission

that came to save them, that brought in measles
and the common cold—the Gabrielinos, they sickened
as the mission prospered, came to own the valley,

carved it up and sold it off, rancho by rancho.
Irrigated, planted to vines, walnuts, oranges,
with prairie-dwellers hurrying in, the ranchos

yet again were subdivided and sold off: a pandemic
frenzy of land changing hands. *The country's mind,
aimed low, grows thick and fat*: thus Emerson,

who looked for such as ravished from the East to rise,
to blaze forth in the West. A West that proved—as
one, musing, would later write—to be, essentially . . .

5

Essentially a customer: thus the exile, musing
of empire's westward course, of intertwinings:
everything is, in a sense (he wrote), *a pattern*

in a carpet. Trodden underfoot. The West
(in short) *was offering nothing.* Whatever
it might choose to take, it took: zeal, doctrine,

manpower: all trodden underfoot. No new thing
usage cannot foul. Who was San Gabriel? Who
thinks of archangels, of angels in Los Angeles?

That winter, while blizzards caromed screaming
over Dakota, Chekhov in Moscow, out of who knows
what stored-up fervor and revulsion, for

the money-fond, obliging Jew who'd tended him,
brought forth a disturbed, disturbing, money-
loathing brother, with his strange smile, so

complex, expressive of such feeling, in which
what predominated was an unfeigned scorn.
February, the tale written and sent off, would see

my father's father with a surveyor's transit,
plotting a tract of greasewood and sagebrush—
desert really. The wells there would soon go dry.

The year is 1888; the place, North Raymond Avenue
in Pasadena. Here, where many still lived under
canvas, in a shake-roofed, newsprint-papered

shack, long since demolished, on the sixth of April—
no doubt yelling as we've all done—my father
entered on a scene of which he'd have no memory.

They'd stay, all told, not quite two years.
How can a descendant, pondering this, not
pause, bemused by the fortuity of things?

The fever runs its course. Less land
changes hands; more wells fail. Jobs dry up.
Hired by a grocer, for six months my father's

father handled accounts, while sick headaches
made his life hell. Eyestrain, he surmised
it was. What was he good for but what

he'd been brought up as, a dirt farmer?
Unless you counted such a thing as friendship.
The best friend, best he'd ever have, would

stay on out there; would, unracked by misgivings,
prosper. The in-laws would likewise trade,
seduced, a banshee-ridden interior winter

for living at the edge, with earthquakes.
Living at the edge, or near it, the Pacific
twenty miles away: in all that time they'd

never seen it. Driving, one day, a hired team
to Long Beach, where the descendants of ten
thousand settlers these days throng, they found

a boardwalk, a cliff above the moiling surf,
the sands. What did it mean, that roaring?
Existences, as they listen and then turn away,

tremble: fate, memory, seaweed-clotted
poluphloisboio thalassēs pouring in immense,
immersing all and every road not taken:

the pagan muse, unwizened, living out there
at the edge, with earthquakes, not to be
counted on. They listen, turn away, head east

toward an interior without a rim, an absence
that can, and does, unsettle—my father's
mother motion-sick, again, much of the way.

6

Years later, even so, they'd go again: the journey
through snowdrifts ending in a blaze of oranges,
the bridged arroyo in winter spate, the in-laws

waiting. With the best friend, said now to be
all business, no time for folks, proving how
a mover and shaker could still remember, talk

deep into the night, as always; passing mention
of unease, something the matter with a kidney;
a last wave from the platform. He'd be dead

within a year. Decades after, my father's father
would ponder that luminous implicit thing,
that bonding. Of how it was, what happened,

the language he groped for is all that's left.
The language, the occasional rhyme and meter:
There crowd my mind . . . His letters, her replies,

that spring he'd turned the sod, off in Dakota,
would one day, as so much foolishness, go
up in smoke. Love letters, another medium

of exchange, burned like the rubles. Chekhov
in 1890 trekked eastward, toward the squalors
of Sakhalin; far from hot baths, item by nit-

encrusted, shivering item, he'd spell out
the exiles' situation. My father's father,
meanwhile, spelled out his own: the eighty

they now lived on, the Dakota tree claim, debts
totaling eight hundred; a wife, two boys, a new-
born daughter. The headaches miserably persisted.

Chekhov would come back spitting blood, with
fourteen years to live. My father's father,
prospering, would acquire more land; eventually

he'd own half a section, put up a house, surround
it with shade trees, an orchard. (My earliest memories
are of that place—an eden of wonder, as though

its secret coves had always been.) He'd be named
county surveyor: chain and compass, plumb bob,
witness trees; lost corners, cemeteries,

culverts, highways. The Louisiana Purchase
pieced and platted, all of it owned. Land-
ownership: the sense of it: he found he liked it.

The headaches did not abate. Behind
the gradual increment of ease, a lurking
hint of something wrong. A twitching

about the neck: What? What? Something was wrong.
A tic, a turning or nodding, an assent or
a denial. As a child, trapped in the doldrums

of Sunday morning, an exile from the modern times
I fervently believed in, I'd observe among
the old ones, the settlers and their shriveling

wives, how many were likewise afflicted.
What did it mean? A giving in to what
could not but be? A judgment? Unwilled

adherence to the devil's party? A sclerosis,
he was told, a hardening about the brain stem.
Mortality stared from within. No, he was told:

the tic was functional, a thing that could
be lived with. He did, for forty years.
Lived anxious, as all animals are anxious:

The stasis between fight and flight. The burrow.
The interminable trilling. Unthinkable,
unthinking space. The distances. The stars.

7

The mysteries of what lived out there, the hunter
and the hunted intertwined; the species that
persisted and that vanished, trodden underfoot:

the linked, perishable, humming webs that only
an unformulating mind could follow, trodden
under: the pattern in the carpet, arabesques

of namelessness, of dreamings; the overlaid
procedure, forethought, accumulation. Assets.
Title deeds. Hot baths. Across the globe,

the neat and fearful grid of settlement. What
stays outside dismissed. Consider the puccoon,
the pasqueflower, the compass plant, the vervain,

as no quasi-monoculture will. Consider the
trout lily, the bluebell and bloodroot my father's
mother brought in from the creekside. A domesticator

born, she made her flowerbeds, her houseplants,
her quilt blocks, her tidy, sunny house the norm:
diffident, adorable, quick to throw up her hands at

what didn't match: "Oh, for the land's sake!"
(What in the world, one wonders now, did that mean?)—
wary of phrases, her love letters expendable:

confront her with what won't come in, won't accept
the settlement: the strange smile of the Jew who
burned the rubles: what then? Imagination

turns, still irresponsible, to Henry James,
a landless, exquisite sort of nomad, who found
no comfort for the dolors of Man Thinking

but in hesitations, velleities, the secret coves
of a surprise the landed, pacing their stiff saraband,
could not have known they harbored: a region

unauthenticated hitherto, awaiting, as
the steppe still did, a muse, a scribe, a bard.
Oh, one can guess what he'd have made of

that strange smile: had he not deemed
Oscar Wilde—who'd die shunned, a rococo
affront to landed propriety—unspeakable?

Chekhov (who wrote plays—that's one connection)
also would die abroad: four years after wild
Oscar; six months after *The Cherry Orchard* opened.

Everything connects, you see: the pattern
in the carpet, trodden underfoot, of Property:
Lopakhin out there hacking at treetrunks:

"Mine! The cherry orchard's mine!" He'd
subdivide it, put up cottages where his forebears, serfs, had felt the knout, where he'd gone

barefoot in winter. . . . No slaves on the prairie, it
may be said. Quite true. A war my great-grandfather
served in saw to that. No chattel slavery—

merely treaties and forced marches. Better the rifle,
some would conclude. Black Hawk's War, the massacre
at Spirit Lake. The losers, what's left of them,

nowadays live on the reservation. That's
what it's called, except by those who live there.
French traders, ransacking their hunting grounds,

called them, from their totem, Renard. They knew
themselves as the Mesquakie. Shunted west to Kansas,
sick, bemused by the black riverbottom land

they'd left, cannily they aped the white man's
game, raised cash, made their bid; signed
papers; moved in; took up the settled life.

8

The settled life: no landed estates, no manors,
no eminences grander than the county courthouse
with its spiked cannon, its humdrum pigeonholes.

Woodlots knot the horizon, pull one in.
The gossip. The scathing whisper. Party lines.
Consensus. Stratifyings: oh yes, even in

a place so nearly level, someone to look
down on—renters; hired men and their unwashed
progeny; the drifter from nowhere; the sinner

found out out of wedlock. Fear of mortgages
foreclosed. Dreams of escape: out of the settled life's
fencerow patrols, into their licensed overthrow:

excess, androgyny, the left wing; anonymity-
celebrity: escape achieved that's no escape,
the waiting misstep, the glassy fjord-leap.

Living anxious. The wind a suicidal howling
in the elevator shaft. The manholes' stinking,
steaming entrails. Dreams, now and again,

lopsided fantasies of going back, weak-kneed,
through the underbrush, and getting even.
One comes to terms, in the long-drawn-out

shadow-war against the old ones: comes
to terms, if one lives long enough, with places
that go strange, that vanish into something else:

is ready to go back, at last, to gravesites, headstones,
the fenced grassland where so many forebears' bones
are boxed and labeled, my grandparents' among them,

my father's and my mother's ashes too. A tranquil
place, unfrightening, now that they rest there:
one comes to terms there, almost, even with dread.

To be landless, half a nomad, nowhere wholly
at home, is to discover, now, an epic theme
in going back. The rootless urge that took

my father's father to Dakota, to California,
impels me there. A settled continent: what
does it mean? I think of nights, half wakeful,

under the roof of their last house, the haven
I knew it as long gone, whoever lives there,
its streetlit solitudes, the clock's tock,

the wooing snuffle of a freight train traveling
along a right of way whose dislodged sleepers now
lie scattered like the bones of mastodons.

I think of Dakota, the wind-raked shelterbelts,
the silos' hived anxiety, the trembling
B-52s. I think of Pasadena: date palms,

hibiscus, pepper trees, the feckless charm
found mainly in the habitat of earthquakes:
half-kempt, aging bungalows gone bridal

under a flowery surfeiting of vines: the desert
fanned, sprinkled, seductive from its bath
of purloined rainbows. North Raymond

not quite a slum; a niggling tenderness
for the outmoded thrives on the scandal
of ways lost, of names gone under. No one

I know or ever heard of lives there now.
On Summit, from some long-obliterated
snapshot, I thought I recognized the house

a great-aunt lived in once: the number
not quite right, the tenant an old
deaf Mexican who did not understand.

NOTES

DALLAS-FORT WORTH: REDBUD AND MISTLETOE

The two quoted passages are from the *Aeneid* of Virgil, translated by Robert Fitzgerald (Random House, 1983, pp. 167 and 79).

MULCIBER AT WEST EGG

From *The Great Gatsby* by F. Scott Fitzgerald (Scribner, 1925, p. 200):
". . . 'They picked him up when he handed the bonds over the counter. They got a circular from New York giving 'em the numbers just five minutes before. What d'you know about that, hey? You never can tell in these hick towns—'
" 'Hello!' I interrupted breathlessly. 'Look here—this isn't Mr. Gatsby. Mr. Gatsby's dead.'
"There was a long silence on the other end of the wire, followed by an exclamation . . . then a quick squawk as the connection was broken.
"I think it was on the third day that a telegram signed Henry C. Gatz arrived from a town in Minnesota. . . ."

AT A REST STOP IN OHIO

An infant wailing in a bus terminal, T. S. Eliot's "Animula" and its sources in the work of Dante and the Emperor Hadrian: this only momentarily surprising conjunction came out of a reading by Howard Nemerov, to whose rendering of *Animula, vagula, blandula* the poem owes its concluding line.

HAVING LUNCH AT BRASENOSE

On Oxford, from *The Blue Guide to England* (Benn, 1980, pp. 274–75): "On the w. side of Radcliff Sq. is Brasenose College, founded in 1509 by Wm. Smyth, Bp. of Lincoln, and Sir Richard Sutton. The name is probably derived from the brazen knocker (a lion's head) of an older Hall, which was carried off to Stamford in 1334; this was recovered in 1890 and is kept in the college hall. Another derivation is from a supposed 'brasenhus' or brewery, on the site of the college."

WESTWARD

From *Civilization: A Personal View*, by Kenneth Clark (Harper & Row, 1969), p. 10:
"Iona was founded by St Columba, who came here from Ireland in the year 543. It seems to have been a sacred spot before he came and for four centuries it was the centre of Celtic Christianity. There are said to have been three hundred and sixty large stone crosses on the island, nearly all of which were thrown into the sea during the Reformation."

A MINOR TREMOR

From Jeremiah 32: 26, 34–35: "Then came the word of the Lord unto Jeremiah, saying: . . . But they set their abominations in the house, which is called by my name, to defile it. And they built the high places of Baal, which are in the valley of the son of Hinnom, to cause their sons and their daughters to pass through the fire unto Moloch; which I commanded them not, neither came it to my mind, that they should do this abomination, to cause Judah to sin."

AMHERST

The profile of Norwottuck, a low hill south of the town of Amherst that would have been familiar to Emily Dickinson, may be viewed from a site, new since her day, honoring graduates of Amherst College who served in the two world wars. The poet's death on May 15, 1886, has been commemorated in recent years by a gathering in the cemetery where she is buried.

Phrases lifted from the poems of Emily Dickinson will be evident. The ones represented include (using the numbers in *The Complete Poems of Emily Dickinson*, edited by Thomas H. Johnson) 526, 530, 663, 595, 658, 594, 601, 564, 593, 486. The most unlikely of these is the poet's reference (in poem 564) to "Vast Prairies of Air/Unbroken by a Settler." Her work is, however, studded with allusions to places she had never seen.

THE HURRICANE AND CHARLOTTE MEW

The devastating windstorm of October 1987, during which countless venerable trees in the south of England were uprooted, appears, according to meteorologists, to have been a strayed Caribbean hurricane. Two poems reprinted in *Charlotte Mew and Her Friends* by Penelope Fitzgerald (Addison-Wesley, 1988), entitled "The Trees Are Down" and "The Shade-Catchers," are the source of several references here.

DEJECTION: A FOOTNOTE

A letter from Samuel Taylor Coleridge to his friend Thomas Poole, dated October 16, 1797, is the source of the incident to which the poem refers.

EASEDALE TARN

From Thomas De Quincey, *Recollections of the Lakes and the Lake Poets* (Penguin, 1985, pp. 250–51): ". . . But there is a third advantage possessed by this Easedale, above other rival valleys, in the sublimity of its mountain barriers. In one of its many rocky recesses is seen a 'force,' (such is the local name for a cataract,) white with foam, descending at all seasons with respectable strength, and, after the melting of snows, with an Alpine violence. Follow the leading of this 'force' for three quarters of a mile, and you come to a little mountain lake, locally termed a 'tarn,' the very finest and most gloomily sublime of its class."

FIREWEED

Known to botanists as *Epilobium angustifolium*, fireweed is so called from its habit of springing up on burnt-over ground, among other unlikely places.

From "Death's Duel," the last sermon preached by John Donne at St. Paul's Cathedral in London: "Whatsoever moved Saint *Jerome* to call the journies of the *Israelites*, in the *wilderness*, Mansions, the word (the word is *Nasang*) signifies but a *journey*, but a peregrination. Even the *Israel of God* hath no mansions; but journies, pilgrimages in this life."

The effigy of John Donne that is to be seen at St. Paul's is one of the few monuments to have survived the great London fire of 1660.

My Cousin Muriel

The needlepoint lace known as *punto in aria*—literally, "a stitch in the air"—originated in Venice, according to the *Columbia Encyclopedia*, as laceworkers ventured beyond purely geometric designs on a ground of netting to freer ones with no ground at all.

Concerning Charles Wadsworth, from *The Life of Emily Dickinson* by Richard B. Sewall (Farrar, Straus & Giroux, 1980, pp. 449–50): "His popularity in Philadelphia has been compared with Henry Ward Beecher's in Brooklyn and his preaching was ranked second only to Beecher's in the country. In April 1862, he accepted a call from the Calvary Presbyterian Society in San Francisco. . . a move which was long thought . . . to account for Emily's complaint . . . of her 'terror since September . . .' In a letter to [Thomas Wentworth] Higginson a few months after Wadsworth died, he was 'my closest earthly friend.' "

The Halloween Parade

From *The Portrait of a Lady*, by Henry James (New American Library, 1979, p. 271): "In the church, as she strolled over its tessellated acres, he was the first person she encountered. She had not been one of the superior tourists who are 'disappointed' in St. Peter's, and find it smaller than its fame; the first time she passed beneath the huge leathern curtain that strains and bangs at the entrance—the first time she found herself beneath the far-arching dome and saw the light drizzle down through the air thickened with incense and with the reflections of marble and gilt, of mosaic and bronze, her conception of greatness received an extension."

Nothing Stays Put

The alstroemeria, like the freesia, is a cultivated flower named presumably for the botanist who first identified or classified it.

The Prairie

Aside from the works of Chekhov and of Emerson quoted in the text, the sources drawn upon here include the privately printed *Some Incidents in My Life: A Saga of the "Unknown" Citizen*, by Frank T. Clampitt; *Iowa: A Bicentennial History*, by Joseph F. Wall (W. W. Norton, 1978); *The Book of the Omaha*, edited by Paul A. Olson (Nebraska Curriculum

Development Center, 1979); and *Pasadena: Crown of the Valley* (Windsor Publications, 1986).

The phrase quoted from George Eliot occurs in *Middlemarch*, Book II, Chapter 20.

Simone Weil wrote in her commentary entitled "The *Iliad*; or The Poem of Force": "Far from hot baths he was indeed, poor man. And not he alone. Nearly all the *Iliad* takes place far from hot baths. Nearly all of human life, then and now, takes place far from hot baths."

The descriptive phrase transliterated here as *poluphloisboio thalassēs* occurs for the first time near the beginning of the *Iliad*. It has been variously handled by translators—from "murmuring" to "loud-roaring" seas and back again. Tennyson perhaps had it in mind when he had his Ulysses say "the deep/Moans round with many voices." Nothing in English, however, comes so close as the Greek to the hissing and tumultuous force of the breaking waves themselves.

ACKNOWLEDGMENTS

Grateful acknowledgment is due to the following periodicals, in which poems appearing in this volume (some in differing versions) were originally published:

Boulevard: "A Minor Tremor," "A Whippoorwill in the Woods"; *The Christian Science Monitor*: "Vacant Lot with Pokeweed"; *The Cream City Review*: "Antiphonal" (under the title "June 24, 1983"), "Mulciber at West Egg"; *The Cresset*: "The Prairie," parts 4 and 5; *Grand Street*: "Amherst," "The Halloween Parade," "Notes on the State of Virginia"; *Gulf Coast*: "Seder Night"; *Lines Review* (Midlothian): "Easedale Tarn," "The Hurricane and Charlotte Mew"; *Literature and Belief*: "The Subway Singer"; *Michigan Quarterly Review*: "Having Lunch at Brasenose," "A Hedge of Rubber Trees"; *The Midwest Quarterly*: "Winter Burial"; *The New Republic*: "Blueberrying in August," "John Donne in California" (under the title "Homesick in Woodside, California"), "Portola Valley"; *The New Yorker*: "Alders," "High Noon," "Meadowlark Country," "My Cousin Muriel," "A Note from Leyden," "Nothing Stays Put," "The Prairie," parts 1–3, "Savannah"; *North Country*: "Grasses"; *Poetry*: "Westward"; *Puckerbrush Review*: "The Beach Pea"; *River Styx*: "Deleted Passage"; *Southwest Review*: "Dallas-Fort Worth: Redbud and Mistletoe," "Iola, Kansas"; *William and Mary Review*: "The Field Pansy"; *The Yale Review*: "Dejection: A Footnote."

"The Subway Singer" also appeared in *Manhattan: Poems and an Elegy*, published in a limited edition by Windhover Press.

"Portola Valley" also appeared in *Ecstatic Occasions, Expedient Forms*, edited by David Lehman (Macmillan, 1987).

"A Minor Tremor" also appeared in *The Best American Poetry, 1989*, edited by Donald Hall (Charles Scribner's Sons, 1989).

For financial support, and for the setting in which some of the work represented in this book was done, the author is indebted to the Academy of American Poets, the American Academy and Institute of Arts and Letters, Amherst College, The College of William and Mary, the Corporation of Yaddo, The Djerassi Foundation, the John Simon Guggenheim Foundation, and Washington University.

A M Y C L A M P I T T was born and brought up in
New Providence, Iowa, graduated from Grinnell
College, and has since lived mainly in New York
City. Her poems began appearing in *The New
Yorker* in 1978, and have since been widely published in magazines and literary journals. Her first
full-length collection, *The Kingfisher*, published in
1983, was followed in 1985 by *What the Light Was
Like*, and in 1987 by *Archaic Figure*. The recipient
in 1982 of a Guggenheim Fellowship and in 1984 of
the fellowship award of the Academy of American
Poets, she is a member of the National Institute of
Arts and Letters, and has been Writer in Residence
at The College of William and Mary, Visiting Writer
at Amherst College, and Visiting Hurst Professor at
Washington University. In June 1987, as that year's
Phi Beta Kappa poet, she read the title poem of this
volume at the Harvard Literary Exercises.

A NOTE ON THE TYPE

The text of this book was set on the Linotype in Fairfield, a typeface designed by the distinguished artist and engraver, Rudolph Ruzicka (1883–1978). Fairfield is the creation of a master craftsman whose type designs exhibit a singular clarity and simplicity which have earned them a permanent place in the typographic repertory.

Ruzicka was born in Bohemia and came to America in 1894. He designed and illustrated many books (including a number for Alfred A. Knopf) and was the creator of a considerable list of individual prints in a variety of techniques.

Composed by Heritage Printers, Inc., Charlotte, North Carolina. Printed and bound by Halliday Lithographers, West Hanover, Massachusetts. Designed by Harry Ford.